THE
WILSON
READING
SYSTEM

STUDENT
READER
FOUR

by Barbara A. Wilson

SECOND EDITION

Wilson Language Training
162 West Main Street
Millbury, Massachusetts 01527-1943
(508) 865-5699

ISBN 1-56778-015-6 8.00 Student Reader Four   Item# SR4

ISBN 1-56778-010-5 33.00 Student Readers 1-6   Item# WRS116

ISBN 1-56778-009-1 78.00 Student Readers 1-12   Item# WRS112

ISBN 1-56778-000-8 196.00 WRS Complete Set   Item# WRS101

The Wilson Reading System is published by:

Wilson Language Training
162 West Main Street
Millbury, MA 01527-1943

Printed in the U.S.A.

S T E P

4

Concepts

4.1   - Vowel - consonant - e syllable in one-syllable words (hope, cave)

4.2   - Vowel - consonant - e syllable combined with closed syllables (combine, baptize)

4.3   - Multisyllabic words combining two syllable types (compensate, illustrate)

4.4   - <u>ive</u> exception: no word ends in v (active, pensive)

lime	quite	hire
code	daze	rope
fake	pole	hate
line	rude	hose
slave	nine	flame

zone	smile	tape
prone	note	flute
blaze	choke	mine
drive	robe	safe
scale	dime	crave

share	tone	ride
joke	drape	plane
chase	scrape	sane
mole	fade	slope
wave	stole	wine

name	mute	sake
drone	dupe	hope
hide	close	glaze
pile	grope	glare
pane	bite	slate

4.1

smoke	stare	white
pride	shame	prune
rise	snake	whale
quote	haze	fire
spade	shine	trade

---

craze	dine	slide
stale	hole	clothe
plate	cane	stake
rule	quake	snipe
poke	spike	tune

---

thrive	shade	flare
rote	spare	late
swipe	flake	rake
tote	shave	gripe
sale	maze	life

scare	blare	yoke
shake	stride	lobe
rite	save	game
lame	stone	strobe
spite	dare	chafe

strikes	snores	hopes
flakes	states	whales
plates	stripes	zones
strokes	hides	quakes
ropes	stores	sites

games	codes	chokes
craves	dives	times
hates	hires	rules
gripes	scones	rakes
pokes	glares	trades

hope	slope	pine
slop	cop	hop
pin	shin	shame
cope	sham	hid
shine	hide	dime

tape	slid	gripe
grip	spite	robe
slide	tap	time
spit	rob	sit
Tim	site	dim

vime	quipe	jire
bode	draze	frope
gake	nole	blate
fline	grude	wose
slive	bine	flome

---

pone	smule	hape
prane	fote	glute
blate	chope	kine
dreve	scobe	dafe
scole	wime	creve

---

shate	*mad* rone	thede
gloke	drope	pline
*fran*chise	screpe	quane
jile	quade	slape
wafe	steke	wike

---

bame	pute	trake
drine	rupe	jope
plide	wose	traze
pite	grepe	plare
glime	shite	thate

    4.1

floke	slare	whike
priche	shime	plune
tise	snade	whope
quope	habe	glire
spame	shune	trode

---

pluze	jine	flide
stathe	fole	clobe
plute	blane	stime
quole	zake	snuke
loke	spive	bune

---

stopes	mipes	priles
flubes	shebes	thrades
chotes	frines	snifes
tefes	vopes	drutes
ploves	scrobes	smotes

---

hefes	sheves	stipes
whokes	prumes	clipes
zepes	quokes	blires
flimes	sipes	trutes
crutes	wames	thomes

4.1

spive	stin	frot
stot	spad	frote
thrap	prete	zin
shike	blire	quim
thepe	chim	quile

---

drene	smip	steke
dren	spale	shope
swite	quate	drim
clem	fush	slep
woth	fushe	triz

---

1. I like the tune that Kate will sing.

2. James did not have a spare when his tire went flat!

3. I hope to make a trade-in for this old van.

4. Jane came down the big slope with Dave.

5. Pete fell off the rise of the big wave.

6. This ham sandwich is bad and the prune cake is stale.

7. There is a snake hole in the mine!

8. If Dale must sit in the shade, I will get a robe.

9. The stale smoke in the club made me ill.

10. We will share the bid to close the contract.

1. Dave will be quite late for the dentist at nine.

2. Kate got lost in the maze of stores in the big mall.

3. Jane got a red linen dress and some silk pants on sale.

4. Tate has lots of pride for his dad.

5. The grandslam left the fans at the game in a daze.

6. Did Jake think that it was rude to stare?

7. The slave was restless to slide in the yoke.

8. Hope did not grope for her cane when she ran from the fire.

9. Mr. Jones held a spade that was trump.

10. Steve Cole has a snapshot of a white whale.

1. Sid has a flute to bring to band class.

2. Beth got pink and white pants on sale at the shop.

3. The spastic child was not safe by himself.

4. Glen put on his robe and sat by the fire.

5. Hank has a limp and must walk with a cane.

6. Did the tot choke on that nut?

7. The dentist felt that Mrs. Smith had the best smile.

8. Dad will drive the kids to tennis class and then go home and take a nap.

9. Let's slide down the slope and then go skate.

10. James will take the flag down off the pole.

4.1

1. Bill intends to shave and dress for the banquet at six p.m.

2. I will ride my fine bike.

3. We can go to the cave next to the lake.

4. Pete must get a spare tire for his van.

5. The bride will sip some white wine at her wedding.

6. Jane will save to get that dress.

7. I suspect that the shop will close at nine.

8. The sun will shine on the pond.

9. If you win the game, you will get a prize.

10. Mr. Jones must hire a consultant to get him out of the mess.

1. Do not choke the pup!

2. The blaze of fire came from the shed.

3. It is a shame that Kate lost her handbag when she was at the mall.

4. After we skate, we will go home.

5. James dove into the cold pond, but Hal and Jane did not.

6. Pete will go on a date with Jan.

7. We can slide on that hill slope.

8. I like that tune and wish it would last.

9. Ed will stoke up the fire and get us a hot drink.

10. It is not safe to chase that red Mustang on the strip.

4.1

1. I got to shake and bake the chops.

2. We will make a cake for Tom.

3. I like it when the sun shines in the den.

4. The lad on the mare made me smile
   when I was sad.

5. The rules in this class are strict.

6. The plum is ripe but the grapes are bad.

7. The man will shake my hand if I take
   the stakes.

8. I like to stroke my cat.

9. When Pete drove into the pole, he ended
   up with whiplash.

10. I plan to attend, but I will be late.

1. I hope to hire Bob Swift, since he is the best man for the job.

2. My dad has to shave and dress.

3. I like to gaze at the sunset and witness the sky at dusk.

4. Steve will tape up his leg for the game.

5. I crave pumpkin pie at lunch.

6. In June, we can swim in the lake.

7. It's such a shame that our mascot will miss the big game.

8. Did Mom ask me to shake the rug?

9. We will dine at home this eve.

10. Dad had to save all his junk, which made Mom upset.

4.1

army
come
have
Mrs.
new
our

1. Mrs. Ross has lots of pride in her children.

2. I do not think that he is quite sane.

3. Did Steve drop chestnuts in the hole of the well?

4. Pete is brave to enlist in the army.

5. Wipe the mess up and come have lunch.

6. Kate will get the shrimp on sale.

7. I hope that I can get a new robe.

8. I do not wish to travel to the cold zone in the state.

9. Can you tell me the name of that dude with the rude kid?

10. The tame mule will take our bags to the home on the lake.

1. Yes, Jane would like a lime in her drink.

2. Kate did not wish to step up on the scale.

3. Can you set the plates and then fill the goblets with wine?

4. Mr. Jones will rise at seven a.m. and get the bus at nine.

5. Beth likes to quote the gossip from the shop.

6. At the end of the trip, Jim did not have a dime left to his name.

7. The punk in the van did not swipe the cash.

8. When they publish the profits, I hope that my stock shares will rise.

9. It will take a long time to wipe this up.

10. Dave did like to scare the kids with his mask.

1. Steve hopes that his stress lessens.

2. Get the stakes for the tent in the van.

3. Pat saves all his cash, but Ellen spends all of her profits.

4. The flames of the fire rose until the sky was lit up.

5. James will not share his bad jokes with us.

6. Dave cuts the grass and then Dale rakes.

7. Justin likes his distinct role at the bank.

8. Ed snores in bed, but he does not think so.

9. The boss states that we must have a more consistent staff.

10. Ted gripes to his pals about the invalid bet.

Hank

Hank sat at home. He did not wish to dine by himself, but his wife, Kate, was on a trip. Hank did crave shrimp. It would be a shame to have an old ham sandwich. It had been a long week, and he wanted to go out.

Hank gave a call to Ted, but Ted had plans. In spite of this, Hank went to the Shrimp Shed. He did not like to dine out by himself, but he did not wish to sit at home. At the Shrimp Shed, Hank met Steve and Beth. He had not seen them for a long time. Steve did ask him to sit and dine with them. Hank was quite glad. Hank made a date with them to get together with Kate.

4.1

Fun With Dad

Dad likes to have fun with his children, Ben and Josh. They are just tots. The kids like to hide on Dad. He has to find them and chase them.

This game was lots of fun, but the kids did not tire and Dad did. Then Dad wore a mask and he hid. Josh and Ben could not find him. At last, he sprang out to scare them, and they went running to Mom. Dad had to take off the mask so they could see it was fake.

The Wire Contract

Jane and Tom had to fix the wires in their old cabin by the lake. They had to hire someone and make a contract for the job. Tom had the name of one man, but he was quite rude. Jane and Tom had time to spare.

At last, they got five quotes. The rude man had given the best quote. Dare they take the risk? Tom and Jane gave the contract to the man with the second best quote. They did not wish to save cash yet end up with a mess.

A Fine Time on the Slope

Stan and Kate like to slide on the hill. It was a fine day to slide with lots of snow on the hill. Stan and Kate got the sleds in the shed. The sun gave the hill a fine shine. The slope was quite big!

Stan and Kate had the sleds at the top of the slope. The sleds went at a fast rate and it was fun. Stan's pet dog ran down the hill after the sleds. Then they had to drag the sleds back up to the top of the slope.

The next time Stan and Kate went down the hill, Stan had a spill! He went into a big snow drift. The crash did not make him stop. He had to brush off the snow, but he strode back up the hill to glide again.

It was late and the sun did fade. They made one last run down the big hill. It was now quite cold on the slope. Stan and Kate had to go home.

At last they got out of the cold. Stan made a fire and Kate went to fix a drink. The fire in the stove was splendid! They had a hot drink and some cake. The day on the slope had been lots of fun.

The Cactus Plant

Mom had lots of plants in her home. Most of them did thrive. Then Jim hid the cactus plant in the drapes. Mom did not miss it.

Jim did not think of the plant and it felt the neglect. The sun did not shine in that spot. It was in the shade and there was a cold draft.

At last Mom saw the cactus plant. There was not much life left to it and she was quite upset! It was just a prank and the neglect had been unintended, but still, mom was mad.

Was there hope for the plant? Mom gave it a sunbath and it came back to life. The cactus was up-lifted and Mom was glad at last.

4.1

The Quake State

In the west, this state is prone to quakes. Yet, in spite of this, people dwell there. In the past, quakes have hit many times. Not much can be done to combat this problem. A quake does not last long, but it is no joke. It can shake things up for miles. The state can be tranquil, and the jilt of a quake can come with a sudden thrust.

People in this zone expect it to happen again. They do not know when it will strike. They can only hope that the impact will not take any homes or victims.

exclude	compare	compose
baseline	tireless	sidestep
nameplate	childlike	flashcube
impure	admire	lineup
oppose	ringside	pulsate

campfire	bobwhite	flagpole
make-up	decade	expose
spitfire	trombone	volume
wineglass	takeoff	on-line
bedtime	immune	hostile

lactose	inhale	rosebud
costume	encase	handshake
fireside	capsize	diffuse
gangrene	crossfire	basement
mandate	shapeless	translate

sidewise	namesake	methane
kingsize	intrude	lifelong
midwife	condone	drive-in
frustrate	fireball	close-up
classmate	escape	transpire

shipmate	confuse	dislike
baseball	statement	insane
whitecap	concrete	basehit
made-up	milkshake	clambake
exhale	fixate	postpone

---

incline	sunstroke	pavement
console	useless	nameless
disrobe	flatware	whitewall
trade-in	postdate	inmate
flagstone	firetrap	state-wide

---

fishplate	telltale	inside
limestone	shameless	umpire
commute	lifetime	timeless
subscribe	filtrate	drugstore
entire	vampire	sidelong

---

welfare	bonfire	enclose
fanfare	sunrise	primrose
lifelike	mistake	software
wildfire	millstone	homeless
sideswipe	offside	yuletide

---

dislike	farewell	sunshine
sidestroke	whalebone	engrave
extreme	stampede	spareribs
unclothe	inquire	pipestem
makeshift	contrive	obscure

---

collide	wineskin	stalemate
self-made	sunbathe	pileup
dispose	wildlife	lifeless
inscribe	off-white	stoneware
transpose	advise	spineless

---

slantwise	membrane	lifeline
ingrate	firebox	contrite
compile	excrete	connive
salesman	sunshade	old-line
dispute	enthrone	ninepins

---

lignite	uptake	tinware
all-time	firebug	milestone
whiteness	brimstone	exude
concave	magnate	obtuse
sideslip	disclose	baptize

---

capsate	inbefe	vilmite
trenzime	dispote	maseplod
transdope	exbale	vennape
conbrile	endame	filkipe
explobe	drenzime	plobbile

disfume	doselit	plebmat
poltrum	glibmax	fretjome
immone	laxtile	oppreve
drenvile	mentrabe	colgrone
pulvene	lebetrom	rettume

1. Kate will complete the job the best that she can.

2. The red rug is in the basement.

3. Can you compute those math problems?

4. I think that it was a mistake to ignore him.

5. Ben must take time to go vote for his classmates.

6. It's fun to sit by the campfire and sing songs.

7. Jan Russel will oppose that bill in congress.

8. The volume of sales went up!

9. Ben will object to that entire plan.

10. I think that Brad will invite Jane to the prom.

1. Jim is tall so he got a kingsize bed.

2. I think that the kids plan to go to the drive-in.

3. This problem does frustrate me!

4. Let's rent that vampire film for the kids.

5. The consultant will advise the staff.

6. Steve and Tom sat by the fireside while Beth and Jan went out on the pond to skate.

7. Frank's old shed is such a firetrap.

8. The console TV will fit in this spot in the den.

9. I like these off-white walls.

10. Dave fell on the flagstone and had to go to the clinic.

1. It upsets me to think of all the homeless people.

2. The infant can not have the lactose in milk.

3. I recommend that we dispose of the old stove.

4. The tots did not wish to admit that it was bedtime.

5. I hate this extreme cold!

6. Mr. Jones did dispute with the umpire during the entire game.

7. The drug addict sold dope to his classmates for cash.

8. Jim is immune to his critics' insults.

9. Ed went to the Shrimp Shed and had a clamplate and a milkshake.

10. We must compare this prospect with the other investments.

1. I bet that the class will dislike this math problem.

2. Dave left for the drugstore to get his pills.

3. Steve had spareribs and kale.

4. Kate made a big mistake to sit by the sunlamp.

5. That software will cost us lots of cash.

6. Ben had to wave farewell to Jane as she got on the nonstop jet to Manhattan.

7. Dad gave Jim a fine handshake.

8. Dave got a big basehit in the sandlot baseball game.

9. The staff had to compile the list of old investments.

10. Mr. Chase did express thanks to his staff in his statement to the press.

1. The gang had a big bonfire for the clambake.

2. Ben had whitewall tires on his red Mustang.

3. If we can win this baseball game, then we will go to the state-wide contest.

4. Pete intended to sit at ringside.

5. Dave Smith will be the umpire for the second game.

6. The contract dispute ended at last.

7. Tom felt like a big milkshake, but Jane just drank a Coke.

8. The gong in the camp rang at sunrise.

9. The old man in this snapshot is your namesake.

10. Steve and Jim had a useless conflict about the job.

1. I hope that we can escape from this damp cave.

2. The men intend to invade the tribe.

3. Dad will not let those kids intrude on the game.

4. Did the stove explode to make such a blast?

5. Let's have a cupcake and some milk.

6. It is a shame that you did not invite Steve and Kate.

7. The van fell into the pothole and got a flat tire.

8. Did you drop this on the pavement?

9. I think that Jane is a fine athlete.

10. We will get more concrete to finish the job.

4.2

1. Pete and Jake will compete in the contest.

2. I do not like to make a mistake.

3. It is bad for your lungs to inhale the smoke.

4. The wire is in the basement.

5. I bet the congressman will win the vote by a landslide.

6. Did you dislike that joke?

7. We must drive to the shop to rent a costume.

8. Dave will inflate the raft and then we can take it out on the lake.

9. I can confide in my wife when I have a problem.

10. Ed had a pancake with his eggs.

Fireside

Tim and Jane sat by the fireside to chat. Tim had a glass of white wine and Jane had an eggnog. Tim had a sip of wine and said, "This is such a fine time to sit by the fire. I must confess, I did think of you last week. I did not expect to see you." Tim lifted the wineskin to fill his glass.

Jane held the cup of eggnog in her hand. "I must admit that I was glad when you did invite me here," she said. "I had to neglect my job a bit to get here, but I did not intend to miss this fine time."

Tim's gaze fell on Jane, and she began to blush. The blaze of the fire was the backdrop for their first kiss.

Complex Math

Tom did not finish his math problems. He did intend to do them before math class, but he could not get them. He was upset. At lunch, he went to Mr. Jones, the math teacher. "I have spent a long time on this and I admit that I cannot get the math," said Tom. "I can subtract, but I cannot get the entire problem."

"Well," said Mr. Jones, "These problems are complex. Jim can help you. He is the best at this. I suspect that lots of kids need help. I intend to do the problems step by step in class."

"Thanks," said Tom. "That is swell. I will ask Jim to help me after I have lunch."

"You will still get credit for it, Tom," said Mr. Jones. "I am glad that you can ask for help when you cannot get the problems. I will see you in class."

In class, Mr. Jones said, "This math is complex! I suspect that many of you had a problem with it."

"Yes!" said Beth and Jeff. "Most of the class did not finish them."

"Well, do not panic. I will do the problems step by step," said Mr. Jones as he gave Tom a wink.

The Limestone Cave

"Will you invite Tom to explore the cave?" asked Beth.

"Yes, I like him. I hope that he can come," said Steve.

Steve and Beth ran to get Tom. Tom felt that it would be fun to explore the limestone cave. Beth, Steve and Tom made plans in the basement of Beth's home.

"Is the cave safe?" asked Steve.

" I think it is. I hope it is!" said Tom.

"Let's take rope, just in case," said Beth.

The next day, they went to the cave. Inside the limestone cave, the rocks were damp. The sun did not shine in the cave. Tom had a flashlight.

"I am brave," said Beth. "Let's go in."

Steve had his hand on the side of the cave. His hand felt something lifelike.

"Shine the flashlight here!" he said.

"What is it?" asked Beth. "Let me see."

"I think it's a bat!" said Steve.

"A bat! That is a bat! Let's go!"

Tom, Beth and Steve left the cave fast. They ran to the lake and fell on the grass.

"We were not brave," said Steve. "I dislike a cave with bats!"

4.2

The Sunshine Club

Kate had to bake for the Sunshine Club. The club met to discuss many topics. The Sunshine Club met on the same date each month.

The club had five past classmates in it. They went to Kate's home unless she could not make it.

Kate did like to chitchat. At times, they would dispute, but the conflict did not last. They had fun and did not gossip. The entire time they would compare notes and explore hundreds of topics. The Sunshine Club was a fine club.

about
Mr.
coach
were
against
team
free

The Big Upset

Ed and Tim have a basketball game against the Tomcats. They had to rush; there was a strict rule about lateness. Mr. Duke, the coach, would explode. Ed was late; he had to tape his leg to compete or he would come up lame. Mr. Duke still let Ed in the game.

The fans were rude to the Tomcats. They wanted them to choke. It was a big game. Ed strode to the line to take the tip. He was not as tall in size, but he was an athlete that could jump. Ed hit the ball to Tim. Tim made a fine shot from the side that did ignite his team.

At the end of the contest, Ed made a pass to Tim in the lane. Then Tim went to the basket. He was hit as a Tomcat made a swipe at the ball. The ball went in and credit was given for the basket. Tim went to the line to take a free shot. The Tomcats had made a big mistake. Tim's shot could win the contest as time would expire. He did not panic and the shot went in! Ed did admire him. The fans did stampede Ed and Tim.

Tim was splendid the entire contest. Ed's game did not compare, but they did combine for twenty baskets to get the upset!

Pothole Problems

Flag St. had a big pothole in the concrete and this was a problem for travel. To drive to West Campus, you had to go on Flag St. Still, the hole went neglected. Then a bus fell in the hole and got a flat tire. This did stop traffic which made people quite upset. It had been a mistake to ignore the problem. Now there was a mess to contend with. The next day, they did fill the hole with gravel, and the pavement was fine again.

administrate	monoxide	atomize
postponement	barehanded	safe-conduct
closefisted	distribute	tranquilize
valentine	life-giving	infantile
compensate	salesmanship	basehitting

incomplete	victimize	custom-made
contribute	sidesplitting	gamesmanship
demonstrate	sidestepping	illustrate
infiltrate	confiscate	Chippendale
recognize	indispose	contemplate

1. Mr. Jones will hire Dave to administrate the West Campus.

2. Steve was closefisted when James made that rude comment.

3. We must find a talented consultant to illustrate the script.

4. The congressman's plans for this district are still incomplete.

5. The vet must tranquilize the pup with a shot.

6. Jake got the K.O. with a barehanded punch.

7. His infantile statement did not escape the press.

8. James must demonstrate his mistake on the math problem.

9. Kate was upset about the postponement of the game.

10. I would like to contribute to Mrs. Smith's bid for Congress.

1. I think that Steve gave Jan a big valentine.

2. Mr. Jones is just sidestepping that big problem, but he will have to address it soon.

3. For the past five games, James has had the best basehitting on the club.

4. Pete would like to get the custom-made chest for Kate.

5. When the boss got back from lunch, the job was still incomplete.

6. Pete's stunt was infantile.

7. We must find a way to compensate for this loss in cash.

8. Jake will help distribute the notes to the class.

9. Can you demonstrate that handshake again?

10. To end the seventh inning, Bill had to grab the pop-up barehanded.

4.3

Valentine for Kate

Bob went on six dates with Kate. He did like her more than the other gals. It was then time to send a valentine. He felt like giving Kate the best valentine yet. He sat to contemplate this.

Bob was talented. He could illustrate quite well. At last he came up with a draft. He made it red and white. It was incomplete, but Bob still had time to finish it.

Bob felt he could make a statement to Kate with this valentine. The kind he could get at a drugstore did not compare! When it was complete, Bob did admire it. This valentine would make Kate glad.

Jane's Pup is Hit

Jane's pup, Spot, was hit by a van on Pride St. Jane had to call her mom to make a postponement of a shopping trip. Then she had to fix a custom-made sling. She felt so sad for the pup and did her best to console him.

Jane went to the pet clinic with Spot in the sling. The vet had to tranquilize him. Jane was restless. At last the vet came out with Spot. The pup did recognize Jane. He would be O.K. Jane felt glad when she saw Spot wag his tail.

massive	captive	inflective
disruptive	attentive	compulsive
intensive	obsessive	connective
impulsive	expensive	passive
subjective	constructive	expansive

---

impressive	inductive	distinctive
effective	extensive	submissive
instinctive	objective	inactive
addictive	subjunctive	expressive
inexpensive	inattentive	affective

---

1.   Steve did not think that Mr. Russel's comments were constructive.

2.   That tot in my class is quite disruptive.

3.   The expansive land for sale in Wisconsin is a wise investment.

4.   We cannot get that expensive console TV.

5.   Congress must pass bills that will stop the sale of that addictive drug.

6.   The script that Pete will publish is quite impressive.

7.   For progress, we must invest in extensive software.

8.   Ben will find a massive hill to slide on.

9.   Beth tends to be a bit compulsive when shopping at the mall.

10.   I was inattentive to that long-winded statement.

1. Mr. Jones will get extensive help from Bob.

2. It is so instinctive for my wellbred dog to hunt.

3. James lost the connective wire for the TV and VCR.

4. Yes, I do think that Gram's muffins are addictive!

5. Beth has the most distinctive smile in the entire class.

6. Kate will help us set the top-most objective for the club.

7. Fred does act just a bit impulsive.

8. I do not think we can fix that massive problem.

9. I hope that the red silk dress is inexpensive so I can get it for the banquet.

10. That French king had an ineffective plan.

The Not-So-Impressive Date

Jake made a date with Beth. She was blond, rich and quite distinctive. He did wish to impress her. Jake got himself expensive pants and a top. He was then set for the big date.

Jake and Beth went to a banquet with Steve and Jan. Jake felt that Beth did like him. Then, all of a sudden, Jake was inattentive. This made him drop his plate of spareribs on his lap. His expensive pants were such a mess. This was not impressive! It made Steve, Jan and Beth poke fun at him.

In the end, Beth gave Jake a big kiss. She did like him with his mess and all! Jake was glad that Beth was not a snob and that she had fun.

4.4

Post Test Step Four

constructive	distribute	whitecap
mine	insane	compensates
sidestepping	adjective	shine
inexpensive	chokes	flatware
clambake	victimize	submissive

---

sheves	zake	fush
glire	scrobes	exbale
vennape	drim	clipes
wames	plobbile	stathe
colgrone	trutes	immone
